BLOG PLA

BLOG TITLE:

DOMAIN:

TARGET AUDIENCE:

NICHE OVERVIEW:

MAIN FOCUS:

PRIMARY KEYWORDS:

MAIN TRAFFIC SOURCES:

BLOG CONTROLS

ADMIN LOGIN:

AFFILIATE ACCOUNTS:

ADVERTISER ACCOUNTS:

HOSTING ACCOUNT LOGIN:

Important Contacts

PARTNERS:

OTHER:

SOCIAL MEDIA

TWITTER

FACEBOOK

INSTAGRAM

PINTEREST

OTHER

OTHER

OTHER

OTHER

BRAND CREATION

SLOGAN / TAGLINE:

WRITING & CONTENT STYLE:

NICHE SUMMARY:

6 WORDS TO DESCRIBE MY BLOG:

HOW MY BLOG PROVIDES VALUE:

MISSION STATEMENT:

BLOG DESIGN

BLOG STYLE IDEAS

THEME USED:

BASE COLOR SCHEME:

PRIMARY FONTS USED:

LOGO / GRAPHIC DESIGNER:

DESIGN CHECKLIST:

- Verify responsive design
- Create 404 landing page
- Install contact form & opt in
- Create advertiser side widgets
- Test links in navigation menu
- Install Cookie Permission Plugin
- Install Privacy Agreement

PLUGIN CHECKLIST:

- Install SEO plugin
- Install WP Total Cache
- Install social sharing plugin
- Install WP Forms
- Install Google Analytics
- Install Backup Plugin
- Install Opt-in Plugin

AFFILIATE INCOME

ADVERTISER ACCOUNTS: **AFFILIATE ACCOUNTS:**

JANUARY

TASKS, MARKETING, ENGAGEMENT & MONETIZATION

CONTENT IDEAS

PROMOTION IDEAS

TOP PRIORITIES

MONTHLY FOCUS

MONETIZATION IDEAS

MONTHLY GOALS

MAIN OBJECTIVE:

GOAL:

ACTION STEPS:

GOAL:

ACTION STEPS:

GOAL:

ACTION STEPS:

TRAFFIC STATS:

MAILING LIST SUBSCRIBERS:

CONTENT PLANNER

POST TITLE:

PUBLICATION DATE:

TARGETED KEYWORDS:

TO DO CHECKLIST:

- Research Topic
- Pinpoint Target Audience
- Choose target keywords
- Optimize for search engines
- Link to other blog post
- Create post images
- Proofread & Edit Post
- Schedule Post Date

SOCIAL SHARING: (circle all that apply)

TOPIC OUTLINE:

NOTES:

CONTENT PLANNER

CATEGORY:

RESOURCE LINKS:

GRAPHICS/IMAGES:

KEY POINTS:

SEO CHECKLIST:

- Primary keyword in post title
- Secondary keyword in sub-title
- Keyword in first paragraph
- Word count > 1000 words
- 1-2 Outbound Links
- Internal Link Structure
- Post URL includes keywords
- Meta description added
- Post includes images
- Post includes sub-headlines
- Social sharing enabled

NOTES:

POST PLANNER

WEEK OF: _____

TYPE: ARTICLE: ☐   TUTORIAL: ☐   REVIEW: ☐   GUEST POST: ☐

PUBLICATION DATE:

TITLE:
CATEGORY:
KEYWORDS:
NOTES:

PUBLICATION DATE:

TITLE:
CATEGORY:
KEYWORDS:
NOTES:

PUBLICATION DATE:

TITLE:
CATEGORY:
KEYWORDS:
NOTES:

POST PLANNER

WEEK OF: _____

TYPE: ARTICLE: ☐   TUTORIAL: ☐   REVIEW: ☐   GUEST POST: ☐

PUBLICATION DATE:

TITLE:

CATEGORY:

KEYWORDS:

NOTES:

LIST BUILDING PROGRESS:

 # SUBSCRIBERS: _____   ☐ **EMAILED THIS WEEK** ✉

SOCIAL MEDIA PROMO THIS WEEK:

☐ Twitter   ☐ Facebook   ☐ Pinterest   ☐ Instagram   ☐ YouTube   ☐ LinkedIn   ☐ Google+

EXTERNAL LINKS:

PRODUCTS PROMOTED:

INTERNAL LINKS:

☐ Affiliate Disclaimer Included

MARKETING PLANNER

TOP TRAFFIC CHANNELS:

MARKETING TO DO LIST:

FREE ADVERTISING IDEAS:

PAID ADVERTISING IDEAS:

MARKETING PLANNER

PROMOTIONAL STRATEGIES TO MAXIMIZE EXPOSURE

PROMOTIONAL IDEAS:

MARKETING TO DO:

SOCIAL MEDIA GROWTH TRACKER:

	BEFORE:	AFTER:
Facebook		
Instagram		
Twitter		
Pinterest		
YouTube		

OTHER:

LIST BUILDING & ENGAGEMENT:

- MAILING LIST SUBSCRIBERS:
- # OF EMAILS SENT TO SUBSCRIBERS:
- # OF NEW BLOG POSTS THIS WEEK:
- # OF COMPLETED GUEST POSTS:

NOTES:

GUEST BLOGGING

POST TITLE:

| PUBLISH DATE: | CATEGORY: |

MAIN TOPIC:

POST SUMMARY:

KEY POINTS:

INCLUDED LINKS:

SHARED ON: FACEBOOK INSTAGRAM TWITTER PINTEREST

TAGS & KEYWORDS:

OF COMMENTS: # OF TRACKBACKS:

NOTES:

FEBRUARY

TASKS, MARKETING, ENGAGEMENT & MONETIZATION

CONTENT IDEAS

PROMOTION IDEAS

TOP PRIORITIES

MONTHLY FOCUS

MONETIZATION IDEAS

MONTHLY GOALS

MAIN OBJECTIVE:

GOAL:

ACTION STEPS:

GOAL:

ACTION STEPS:

GOAL:

ACTION STEPS:

TRAFFIC STATS:

MAILING LIST SUBSCRIBERS:

CONTENT PLANNER

POST TITLE:

TARGETED KEYWORDS:

SOCIAL SHARING: (circle all that apply)

TOPIC OUTLINE:

PUBLICATION DATE:

TO DO CHECKLIST:

- Research Topic
- Pinpoint Target Audience
- Choose target keywords
- Optimize for search engines
- Link to other blog post
- Create post images
- Proofread & Edit Post
- Schedule Post Date

NOTES:

CONTENT PLANNER

CATEGORY:

RESOURCE LINKS:

GRAPHICS/IMAGES:

KEY POINTS:

SEO CHECKLIST:

- Primary keyword in post title
- Secondary keyword in sub-title
- Keyword in first paragraph
- Word count > 1000 words
- 1-2 Outbound Links
- Internal Link Structure
- Post URL includes keywords
- Meta description added
- Post includes images
- Post includes sub-headlines
- Social sharing enabled

NOTES:

POST PLANNER

WEEK OF: _____

TYPE: ARTICLE: ☐ TUTORIAL: ☐ REVIEW: ☐ GUEST POST: ☐

PUBLICATION DATE:

TITLE: _____
CATEGORY: _____
KEYWORDS: _____
NOTES: _____

PUBLICATION DATE:

TITLE: _____
CATEGORY: _____
KEYWORDS: _____
NOTES: _____

PUBLICATION DATE:

TITLE: _____
CATEGORY: _____
KEYWORDS: _____
NOTES: _____

POST PLANNER

WEEK OF: _____

TYPE: ARTICLE: TUTORIAL: REVIEW: GUEST POST:

PUBLICATION DATE:

TITLE:

CATEGORY:

KEYWORDS:

NOTES:

LIST BUILDING PROGRESS:

 # SUBSCRIBERS: **EMAILED THIS WEEK** ✉

SOCIAL MEDIA PROMO THIS WEEK:

Twitter   Facebook   Pinterest   Instagram   YouTube   LinkedIn   Google+

EXTERNAL LINKS: **PRODUCTS PROMOTED:**

INTERNAL LINKS:

Affiliate Disclaimer Included

POST PLANNER

WEEK OF: _____

TYPE: ARTICLE: ☐   TUTORIAL: ☐   REVIEW: ☐   GUEST POST: ☐

PUBLICATION DATE:

TITLE:

CATEGORY:

KEYWORDS:

NOTES:

LIST BUILDING PROGRESS:

 # SUBSCRIBERS: _____   **EMAILED THIS WEEK** ✉

SOCIAL MEDIA PROMO THIS WEEK:

☐ Twitter   ☐ Facebook   ☐ Pinterest   ☐ Instagram   ☐ YouTube   ☐ LinkedIn   ☐ Google+

EXTERNAL LINKS:

PRODUCTS PROMOTED:

INTERNAL LINKS:

☐ Affiliate Disclaimer Included

MARKETING PLANNER

TOP TRAFFIC CHANNELS:

MARKETING TO DO LIST:

FREE ADVERTISING IDEAS:

PAID ADVERTISING IDEAS:

MARKETING PLANNER

PROMOTIONAL STRATEGIES TO MAXIMIZE EXPOSURE

PROMOTIONAL IDEAS:

MARKETING TO DO:

SOCIAL MEDIA GROWTH TRACKER:

	BEFORE:	AFTER:
Facebook		
Instagram		
Twitter		
Pinterest		
YouTube		

OTHER:

LIST BUILDING & ENGAGEMENT:

- **MAILING LIST SUBSCRIBERS:**
- **# OF EMAILS SENT TO SUBSCRIBERS:**
- **# OF NEW BLOG POSTS THIS WEEK:**
- **# OF COMPLETED GUEST POSTS:**

NOTES:

GUEST BLOGGING

POST TITLE:

PUBLISH DATE:	CATEGORY:
MAIN TOPIC:	
POST SUMMARY:	

KEY POINTS:

INCLUDED LINKS:

SHARED ON:
- FACEBOOK
- INSTAGRAM
- TWITTER
- PINTEREST

TAGS & KEYWORDS:

 # OF COMMENTS: **# OF TRACKBACKS:**

NOTES:

MARCH

TASKS, MARKETING, ENGAGEMENT & MONETIZATION

CONTENT IDEAS

PROMOTION IDEAS

TOP PRIORITIES

MONTHLY FOCUS

MONETIZATION IDEAS

MONTHLY GOALS

MAIN OBJECTIVE:

GOAL:

ACTION STEPS:

GOAL:

ACTION STEPS:

GOAL:

ACTION STEPS:

TRAFFIC STATS:

MAILING LIST SUBSCRIBERS:

CONTENT PLANNER

POST TITLE:

PUBLICATION DATE:

TARGETED KEYWORDS:

TO DO CHECKLIST:

- Research Topic
- Pinpoint Target Audience
- Choose target keywords
- Optimize for search engines
- Link to other blog post
- Create post images
- Proofread & Edit Post
- Schedule Post Date

SOCIAL SHARING: (circle all that apply)

Facebook Twitter YouTube Pinterest LinkedIn Instagram

TOPIC OUTLINE:

NOTES:

CONTENT PLANNER

CATEGORY:

RESOURCE LINKS:

GRAPHICS/IMAGES:

KEY POINTS:

SEO CHECKLIST:

- Primary keyword in post title
- Secondary keyword in sub-title
- Keyword in first paragraph
- Word count > 1000 words
- 1-2 Outbound Links
- Internal Link Structure
- Post URL includes keywords
- Meta description added
- Post includes images
- Post includes sub-headlines
- Social sharing enabled

NOTES:

POST PLANNER

WEEK OF: _____

TYPE: ARTICLE: ☐   TUTORIAL: ☐   REVIEW: ☐   GUEST POST: ☐

PUBLICATION DATE:

TITLE:

CATEGORY:

KEYWORDS:

NOTES:

PUBLICATION DATE:

TITLE:

CATEGORY:

KEYWORDS:

NOTES:

PUBLICATION DATE:

TITLE:

CATEGORY:

KEYWORDS:

NOTES:

POST PLANNER

WEEK OF: _____

TYPE: ARTICLE: ☐   TUTORIAL: ☐   REVIEW: ☐   GUEST POST: ☐

PUBLICATION DATE:

TITLE:

CATEGORY:

KEYWORDS:

NOTES:

LIST BUILDING PROGRESS:

SUBSCRIBERS: EMAILED THIS WEEK ✉

SOCIAL MEDIA PROMO THIS WEEK:

☐ Twitter   ☐ Facebook   ☐ Pinterest   ☐ Instagram   ☐ YouTube   ☐ LinkedIn   ☐ Google+

EXTERNAL LINKS:

PRODUCTS PROMOTED:

INTERNAL LINKS:

Affiliate Disclaimer Included

POST PLANNER

WEEK OF: _____

TYPE: ARTICLE: ☐   TUTORIAL: ☐   REVIEW: ☐   GUEST POST: ☐

PUBLICATION DATE:

TITLE:

CATEGORY:

KEYWORDS:

NOTES:

LIST BUILDING PROGRESS:

 # SUBSCRIBERS: _____   **EMAILED THIS WEEK** ✉

SOCIAL MEDIA PROMO THIS WEEK:

☐ Twitter   ☐ Facebook   ☐ Pinterest   ☐ Instagram   ☐ YouTube   ☐ LinkedIn   ☐ Google+

EXTERNAL LINKS:

PRODUCTS PROMOTED:

INTERNAL LINKS:

☐ Affiliate Disclaimer Included

MARKETING PLANNER

TOP TRAFFIC CHANNELS:

MARKETING TO DO LIST:

FREE ADVERTISING IDEAS:

PAID ADVERTISING IDEAS:

MARKETING PLANNER

PROMOTIONAL STRATEGIES TO MAXIMIZE EXPOSURE

PROMOTIONAL IDEAS:

MARKETING TO DO:

SOCIAL MEDIA GROWTH TRACKER:

	BEFORE:	AFTER:
Facebook		
Instagram		
Twitter		
Pinterest		
YouTube		

OTHER:

LIST BUILDING & ENGAGEMENT:

MAILING LIST SUBSCRIBERS:

OF EMAILS SENT TO SUBSCRIBERS:

OF NEW BLOG POSTS THIS WEEK:

OF COMPLETED GUEST POSTS:

NOTES:

GUEST BLOGGING

POST TITLE:

PUBLISH DATE:

CATEGORY:

MAIN TOPIC:

POST SUMMARY:

KEY POINTS:

INCLUDED LINKS:

SHARED ON:
FACEBOOK   INSTAGRAM
TWITTER   PINTEREST

TAGS & KEYWORDS:

OF COMMENTS: # OF TRACKBACKS:

NOTES:

APRIL

TASKS, MARKETING, ENGAGEMENT & MONETIZATION

CONTENT IDEAS

PROMOTION IDEAS

TOP PRIORITIES

MONTHLY FOCUS

MONETIZATION IDEAS

MONTHLY GOALS

MAIN OBJECTIVE:

GOAL:

ACTION STEPS:

GOAL:

ACTION STEPS:

GOAL:

ACTION STEPS:

TRAFFIC STATS:

MAILING LIST SUBSCRIBERS:

CONTENT PLANNER

POST TITLE:

PUBLICATION DATE:

TARGETED KEYWORDS:

TO DO CHECKLIST:

- Research Topic
- Pinpoint Target Audience
- Choose target keywords
- Optimize for search engines
- Link to other blog post
- Create post images
- Proofread & Edit Post
- Schedule Post Date

SOCIAL SHARING: (circle all that apply)

Facebook Twitter YouTube Pinterest LinkedIn Instagram

TOPIC OUTLINE:

NOTES:

CONTENT PLANNER

CATEGORY:

RESOURCE LINKS:

GRAPHICS/IMAGES:

KEY POINTS:

SEO CHECKLIST:

- Primary keyword in post title
- Secondary keyword in sub-title
- Keyword in first paragraph
- Word count > 1000 words
- 1-2 Outbound Links
- Internal Link Structure
- Post URL includes keywords
- Meta description added
- Post includes images
- Post includes sub-headlines
- Social sharing enabled

NOTES:

POST PLANNER

WEEK OF: _____

TYPE: ARTICLE: ☐   TUTORIAL: ☐   REVIEW: ☐   GUEST POST: ☐

PUBLICATION DATE:

TITLE:

CATEGORY:

KEYWORDS:

NOTES:

PUBLICATION DATE:

TITLE:

CATEGORY:

KEYWORDS:

NOTES:

PUBLICATION DATE:

TITLE:

CATEGORY:

KEYWORDS:

NOTES:

POST PLANNER

WEEK OF: _____

TYPE: ARTICLE: ☐   TUTORIAL: ☐   REVIEW: ☐   GUEST POST: ☐

PUBLICATION DATE:

TITLE:

CATEGORY:

KEYWORDS:

NOTES:

LIST BUILDING PROGRESS:

 # SUBSCRIBERS: **EMAILED THIS WEEK** ✉

SOCIAL MEDIA PROMO THIS WEEK:

☐ Twitter   ☐ Facebook   ☐ Pinterest   ☐ Instagram   ☐ YouTube   ☐ LinkedIn   ☐ Google+

EXTERNAL LINKS: **PRODUCTS PROMOTED:**

INTERNAL LINKS:

Affiliate Disclaimer Included

POST PLANNER

WEEK OF: _____

TYPE: ARTICLE: ☐   TUTORIAL: ☐   REVIEW: ☐   GUEST POST: ☐

PUBLICATION DATE:

TITLE:
CATEGORY:
KEYWORDS:
NOTES:

LIST BUILDING PROGRESS:

SUBSCRIBERS: _____   EMAILED THIS WEEK ✉

SOCIAL MEDIA PROMO THIS WEEK:

☐ Twitter   ☐ Facebook   ☐ Pinterest   ☐ Instagram   ☐ YouTube   ☐ LinkedIn   ☐ Google+

EXTERNAL LINKS:

INTERNAL LINKS:

PRODUCTS PROMOTED:

☐ Affiliate Disclaimer Included

MARKETING PLANNER

TOP TRAFFIC CHANNELS:

MARKETING TO DO LIST:

FREE ADVERTISING IDEAS:

PAID ADVERTISING IDEAS:

MARKETING PLANNER

PROMOTIONAL STRATEGIES TO MAXIMIZE EXPOSURE

PROMOTIONAL IDEAS:

MARKETING TO DO:

SOCIAL MEDIA GROWTH TRACKER:

	BEFORE:	AFTER:
Facebook		
Instagram		
Twitter		
Pinterest		
YouTube		

OTHER:

LIST BUILDING & ENGAGEMENT:

MAILING LIST SUBSCRIBERS:

 # OF EMAILS SENT TO SUBSCRIBERS:

 # OF NEW BLOG POSTS THIS WEEK:

 # OF COMPLETED GUEST POSTS:

NOTES:

GUEST BLOGGING

POST TITLE:

PUBLISH DATE:

CATEGORY:

MAIN TOPIC:

POST SUMMARY:

KEY POINTS:

INCLUDED LINKS:

SHARED ON:
- FACEBOOK
- INSTAGRAM
- TWITTER
- PINTEREST

TAGS & KEYWORDS:

OF COMMENTS:

OF TRACKBACKS:

NOTES:

MAY

TASKS, MARKETING, ENGAGEMENT & MONETIZATION

CONTENT IDEAS

PROMOTION IDEAS

TOP PRIORITIES

MONTHLY FOCUS

MONETIZATION IDEAS

MONTHLY GOALS

MAIN OBJECTIVE:

GOAL:

ACTION STEPS:

GOAL:

ACTION STEPS:

GOAL:

ACTION STEPS:

TRAFFIC STATS:

MAILING LIST SUBSCRIBERS:

CONTENT PLANNER

POST TITLE:

TARGETED KEYWORDS:

SOCIAL SHARING: (circle all that apply)

f twitter youtube pinterest in instagram

TOPIC OUTLINE:

PUBLICATION DATE:

TO DO CHECKLIST:

- Research Topic
- Pinpoint Target Audience
- Choose target keywords
- Optimize for search engines
- Link to other blog post
- Create post images
- Proofread & Edit Post
- Schedule Post Date

NOTES:

CONTENT PLANNER

CATEGORY:

RESOURCE LINKS:

GRAPHICS/IMAGES:

KEY POINTS:

SEO CHECKLIST:

- Primary keyword in post title
- Secondary keyword in sub-title
- Keyword in first paragraph
- Word count > 1000 words
- 1-2 Outbound Links
- Internal Link Structure
- Post URL includes keywords
- Meta description added
- Post includes images
- Post includes sub-headlines
- Social sharing enabled

NOTES:

POST PLANNER

WEEK OF: _____

TYPE: ARTICLE: ☐   TUTORIAL: ☐   REVIEW: ☐   GUEST POST: ☐

PUBLICATION DATE:

TITLE:

CATEGORY:

KEYWORDS:

NOTES:

PUBLICATION DATE:

TITLE:

CATEGORY:

KEYWORDS:

NOTES:

PUBLICATION DATE:

TITLE:

CATEGORY:

KEYWORDS:

NOTES:

POST PLANNER

WEEK OF: _____

TYPE: ARTICLE: ☐   TUTORIAL: ☐   REVIEW: ☐   GUEST POST: ☐

PUBLICATION DATE:

TITLE: _____
CATEGORY: _____
KEYWORDS: _____
NOTES:

LIST BUILDING PROGRESS:

SUBSCRIBERS: _____   **EMAILED THIS WEEK** ✉

SOCIAL MEDIA PROMO THIS WEEK:

☐ Twitter   ☐ Facebook   ☐ Pinterest   ☐ Instagram   ☐ YouTube   ☐ LinkedIn   ☐ Google+

EXTERNAL LINKS:

PRODUCTS PROMOTED:

INTERNAL LINKS:

☐ Affiliate Disclaimer Included

POST PLANNER

WEEK OF: _____

TYPE: ARTICLE: ☐   TUTORIAL: ☐   REVIEW: ☐   GUEST POST: ☐

PUBLICATION DATE:

TITLE:

CATEGORY:

KEYWORDS:

NOTES:

LIST BUILDING PROGRESS:

SUBSCRIBERS: _____   EMAILED THIS WEEK ✉

SOCIAL MEDIA PROMO THIS WEEK:

☐ Twitter   ☐ Facebook   ☐ Pinterest   ☐ Instagram   ☐ YouTube   ☐ LinkedIn   ☐ Google+

EXTERNAL LINKS:

PRODUCTS PROMOTED:

INTERNAL LINKS:

☐ Affiliate Disclaimer Included

MARKETING PLANNER

TOP TRAFFIC CHANNELS:

MARKETING TO DO LIST:

FREE ADVERTISING IDEAS:

PAID ADVERTISING IDEAS:

MARKETING PLANNER

PROMOTIONAL STRATEGIES TO MAXIMIZE EXPOSURE

PROMOTIONAL IDEAS:

MARKETING TO DO:

SOCIAL MEDIA GROWTH TRACKER:

	BEFORE:	AFTER:
Facebook		
Instagram		
Twitter		
Pinterest		
YouTube		

OTHER:

LIST BUILDING & ENGAGEMENT:

- MAILING LIST SUBSCRIBERS:
- # OF EMAILS SENT TO SUBSCRIBERS:
- # OF NEW BLOG POSTS THIS WEEK:
- # OF COMPLETED GUEST POSTS:

NOTES:

GUEST BLOGGING

POST TITLE:

PUBLISH DATE:	CATEGORY:
MAIN TOPIC:	
POST SUMMARY:	

KEY POINTS:

INCLUDED LINKS:

SHARED ON:
- FACEBOOK
- INSTAGRAM
- TWITTER
- PINTEREST

TAGS & KEYWORDS:

 # OF COMMENTS:

 # OF TRACKBACKS:

NOTES:

JUNE

TASKS, MARKETING, ENGAGEMENT & MONETIZATION

CONTENT IDEAS

PROMOTION IDEAS

TOP PRIORITIES

MONTHLY FOCUS

MONETIZATION IDEAS

MONTHLY GOALS

MAIN OBJECTIVE:

GOAL:

ACTION STEPS:

GOAL:

ACTION STEPS:

GOAL:

ACTION STEPS:

TRAFFIC STATS:

MAILING LIST SUBSCRIBERS:

CONTENT PLANNER

POST TITLE:

PUBLICATION DATE:

TARGETED KEYWORDS:

TO DO CHECKLIST:

- Research Topic
- Pinpoint Target Audience
- Choose target keywords
- Optimize for search engines
- Link to other blog post
- Create post images
- Proofread & Edit Post
- Schedule Post Date

SOCIAL SHARING: (circle all that apply)

Facebook Twitter YouTube Pinterest LinkedIn Instagram

TOPIC OUTLINE:

NOTES:

CONTENT PLANNER

CATEGORY:

RESOURCE LINKS:

GRAPHICS/IMAGES:

KEY POINTS:

SEO CHECKLIST:

- Primary keyword in post title
- Secondary keyword in sub-title
- Keyword in first paragraph
- Word count > 1000 words
- 1-2 Outbound Links
- Internal Link Structure
- Post URL includes keywords
- Meta description added
- Post includes images
- Post includes sub-headlines
- Social sharing enabled

NOTES:

POST PLANNER

WEEK OF: _____

TYPE: ARTICLE: ☐   TUTORIAL: ☐   REVIEW: ☐   GUEST POST: ☐

PUBLICATION DATE:

TITLE:
CATEGORY:
KEYWORDS:
NOTES:

PUBLICATION DATE:

TITLE:
CATEGORY:
KEYWORDS:
NOTES:

PUBLICATION DATE:

TITLE:
CATEGORY:
KEYWORDS:
NOTES:

POST PLANNER

WEEK OF: _____

TYPE: ARTICLE: ☐   TUTORIAL: ☐   REVIEW: ☐   GUEST POST: ☐

PUBLICATION DATE:

TITLE:
CATEGORY:
KEYWORDS:
NOTES:

LIST BUILDING PROGRESS:

 # SUBSCRIBERS: _____   **EMAILED THIS WEEK** ✉

SOCIAL MEDIA PROMO THIS WEEK:

Twitter ☐   Facebook ☐   Pinterest ☐   Instagram ☐   YouTube ☐   LinkedIn ☐   Google+ ☐

EXTERNAL LINKS:

PRODUCTS PROMOTED:

INTERNAL LINKS:

Affiliate Disclaimer Included

POST PLANNER

WEEK OF: _____

TYPE: ARTICLE: ☐   TUTORIAL: ☐   REVIEW: ☐   GUEST POST: ☐

PUBLICATION DATE:

TITLE:
CATEGORY:
KEYWORDS:
NOTES:

LIST BUILDING PROGRESS:

 # SUBSCRIBERS: _____   **EMAILED THIS WEEK** ✉

SOCIAL MEDIA PROMO THIS WEEK:

☐ Twitter ☐ Facebook ☐ Pinterest ☐ Instagram ☐ YouTube ☐ LinkedIn ☐ Google+

EXTERNAL LINKS:

PRODUCTS PROMOTED:

INTERNAL LINKS:

☐ Affiliate Disclaimer Included

MARKETING PLANNER

TOP TRAFFIC CHANNELS:

MARKETING TO DO LIST:

FREE ADVERTISING IDEAS:

PAID ADVERTISING IDEAS:

MARKETING PLANNER

PROMOTIONAL STRATEGIES TO MAXIMIZE EXPOSURE

PROMOTIONAL IDEAS:

MARKETING TO DO:

SOCIAL MEDIA GROWTH TRACKER:

	BEFORE:	AFTER:
Facebook		
Instagram		
Twitter		
Pinterest		
YouTube		

OTHER:

LIST BUILDING & ENGAGEMENT:

MAILING LIST SUBSCRIBERS:	
# OF EMAILS SENT TO SUBSCRIBERS:	
# OF NEW BLOG POSTS THIS WEEK:	
# OF COMPLETED GUEST POSTS:	

NOTES:

GUEST BLOGGING

POST TITLE:

PUBLISH DATE:	CATEGORY:
MAIN TOPIC:	
POST SUMMARY:	

KEY POINTS:

INCLUDED LINKS:

SHARED ON:
- FACEBOOK
- INSTAGRAM
- TWITTER
- PINTEREST

TAGS & KEYWORDS:

OF COMMENTS:

OF TRACKBACKS:

NOTES:

JULY

TASKS, MARKETING, ENGAGEMENT & MONETIZATION

CONTENT IDEAS

PROMOTION IDEAS

TOP PRIORITIES

MONTHLY FOCUS

MONETIZATION IDEAS

MONTHLY GOALS

MAIN OBJECTIVE:

GOAL:

ACTION STEPS:

GOAL:

ACTION STEPS:

GOAL:

ACTION STEPS:

TRAFFIC STATS:

MAILING LIST SUBSCRIBERS:

CONTENT PLANNER

POST TITLE:

PUBLICATION DATE:

TARGETED KEYWORDS:

TO DO CHECKLIST:

- Research Topic
- Pinpoint Target Audience
- Choose target keywords
- Optimize for search engines
- Link to other blog post
- Create post images
- Proofread & Edit Post
- Schedule Post Date

SOCIAL SHARING: (circle all that apply)

Facebook Twitter YouTube Pinterest LinkedIn Instagram

TOPIC OUTLINE:

NOTES:

CONTENT PLANNER

CATEGORY:

RESOURCE LINKS:

GRAPHICS/IMAGES:

KEY POINTS:

SEO CHECKLIST:

- Primary keyword in post title
- Secondary keyword in sub-title
- Keyword in first paragraph
- Word count > 1000 words
- 1-2 Outbound Links
- Internal Link Structure
- Post URL includes keywords
- Meta description added
- Post includes images
- Post includes sub-headlines
- Social sharing enabled

NOTES:

POST PLANNER

WEEK OF: _____

TYPE: ARTICLE: ☐   TUTORIAL: ☐   REVIEW: ☐   GUEST POST: ☐

PUBLICATION DATE:

TITLE: _____

CATEGORY: _____

KEYWORDS: _____

NOTES: _____

PUBLICATION DATE:

TITLE: _____

CATEGORY: _____

KEYWORDS: _____

NOTES: _____

PUBLICATION DATE:

TITLE: _____

CATEGORY: _____

KEYWORDS: _____

NOTES: _____

POST PLANNER

WEEK OF: _____

TYPE: ARTICLE: ☐   TUTORIAL: ☐   REVIEW: ☐   GUEST POST: ☐

PUBLICATION DATE:

TITLE:

CATEGORY:

KEYWORDS:

NOTES:

LIST BUILDING PROGRESS:

 # SUBSCRIBERS: **EMAILED THIS WEEK** ✉

SOCIAL MEDIA PROMO THIS WEEK:

🐦   f   P   📷   ▶   in   g+

EXTERNAL LINKS:

PRODUCTS PROMOTED:

INTERNAL LINKS:

Affiliate Disclaimer Included

MARKETING PLANNER

TOP TRAFFIC CHANNELS:

MARKETING TO DO LIST:

FREE ADVERTISING IDEAS:

PAID ADVERTISING IDEAS:

MARKETING PLANNER

PROMOTIONAL STRATEGIES TO MAXIMIZE EXPOSURE

PROMOTIONAL IDEAS:

MARKETING TO DO:

SOCIAL MEDIA GROWTH TRACKER:

	BEFORE:	AFTER:
f		
📷		
🐦		
P		
▶		

OTHER:

LIST BUILDING & ENGAGEMENT:

MAILING LIST SUBSCRIBERS:

 # OF EMAILS SENT TO SUBSCRIBERS:

 # OF NEW BLOG POSTS THIS WEEK:

 # OF COMPLETED GUEST POSTS:

NOTES:

GUEST BLOGGING

POST TITLE:

PUBLISH DATE:	CATEGORY:

MAIN TOPIC:

POST SUMMARY:

KEY POINTS:

INCLUDED LINKS:

SHARED ON: FACEBOOK | INSTAGRAM | TWITTER | PINTEREST

TAGS & KEYWORDS:

OF COMMENTS: | # OF TRACKBACKS:

NOTES:

AUGUST

TASKS, MARKETING, ENGAGEMENT & MONETIZATION

CONTENT IDEAS

PROMOTION IDEAS

TOP PRIORITIES

MONTHLY FOCUS

MONETIZATION IDEAS

MONTHLY GOALS

MAIN OBJECTIVE:

GOAL:

ACTION STEPS:

GOAL:

ACTION STEPS:

GOAL:

ACTION STEPS:

TRAFFIC STATS:

MAILING LIST SUBSCRIBERS:

CONTENT PLANNER

POST TITLE:

PUBLICATION DATE:

TARGETED KEYWORDS:

TO DO CHECKLIST:

- Research Topic
- Pinpoint Target Audience
- Choose target keywords
- Optimize for search engines
- Link to other blog post
- Create post images
- Proofread & Edit Post
- Schedule Post Date

SOCIAL SHARING: (circle all that apply)

facebook twitter youtube pinterest linkedin instagram

TOPIC OUTLINE:

NOTES:

CONTENT PLANNER

CATEGORY:

RESOURCE LINKS:

GRAPHICS/IMAGES:

KEY POINTS:

SEO CHECKLIST:

- Primary keyword in post title
- Secondary keyword in sub-title
- Keyword in first paragraph
- Word count > 1000 words
- 1-2 Outbound Links
- Internal Link Structure
- Post URL includes keywords
- Meta description added
- Post includes images
- Post includes sub-headlines
- Social sharing enabled

NOTES:

POST PLANNER

WEEK OF: _____

TYPE: ARTICLE: TUTORIAL: REVIEW: GUEST POST:

PUBLICATION DATE:

TITLE:

CATEGORY:

KEYWORDS:

NOTES:

PUBLICATION DATE:

TITLE:

CATEGORY:

KEYWORDS:

NOTES:

PUBLICATION DATE:

TITLE:

CATEGORY:

KEYWORDS:

NOTES:

POST PLANNER

WEEK OF: _____

TYPE: ARTICLE: ☐   TUTORIAL: ☐   REVIEW: ☐   GUEST POST: ☐

PUBLICATION DATE:

TITLE:

CATEGORY:

KEYWORDS:

NOTES:

LIST BUILDING PROGRESS:

 # SUBSCRIBERS: _____   **EMAILED THIS WEEK** ✉

SOCIAL MEDIA PROMO THIS WEEK:

☐ Twitter   ☐ Facebook   ☐ Pinterest   ☐ Instagram   ☐ YouTube   ☐ LinkedIn   ☐ Google+

EXTERNAL LINKS:

PRODUCTS PROMOTED:

INTERNAL LINKS:

☐ Affiliate Disclaimer Included

MARKETING PLANNER

TOP TRAFFIC CHANNELS:

MARKETING TO DO LIST:

FREE ADVERTISING IDEAS:

PAID ADVERTISING IDEAS:

MARKETING PLANNER

PROMOTIONAL STRATEGIES TO MAXIMIZE EXPOSURE

PROMOTIONAL IDEAS:

MARKETING TO DO:

SOCIAL MEDIA GROWTH TRACKER:

BEFORE: AFTER:

- Facebook
- Instagram
- Twitter
- Pinterest
- YouTube

OTHER:

LIST BUILDING & ENGAGEMENT:

MAILING LIST SUBSCRIBERS:

OF EMAILS SENT TO SUBSCRIBERS:

OF NEW BLOG POSTS THIS WEEK:

OF COMPLETED GUEST POSTS:

NOTES:

GUEST BLOGGING

POST TITLE:

PUBLISH DATE:

CATEGORY:

MAIN TOPIC:

POST SUMMARY:

KEY POINTS:

INCLUDED LINKS:

SHARED ON:
FACEBOOK   INSTAGRAM
TWITTER   PINTEREST

TAGS & KEYWORDS:

OF COMMENTS: # OF TRACKBACKS:

NOTES:

SEPTEMBER

TASKS, MARKETING, ENGAGEMENT & MONETIZATION

CONTENT IDEAS

PROMOTION IDEAS

TOP PRIORITIES

MONTHLY FOCUS

MONETIZATION IDEAS

MONTHLY GOALS

MAIN OBJECTIVE:

GOAL:

ACTION STEPS:

GOAL:

ACTION STEPS:

GOAL:

ACTION STEPS:

TRAFFIC STATS:

MAILING LIST SUBSCRIBERS:

CONTENT PLANNER

POST TITLE:

TARGETED KEYWORDS:

SOCIAL SHARING: (circle all that apply)

Facebook Twitter YouTube Pinterest LinkedIn Instagram

TOPIC OUTLINE:

PUBLICATION DATE:

TO DO CHECKLIST:

- ☐ Research Topic
- ☐ Pinpoint Target Audience
- ☐ Choose target keywords
- ☐ Optimize for search engines
- ☐ Link to other blog post
- ☐ Create post images
- ☐ Proofread & Edit Post
- ☐ Schedule Post Date

NOTES:

CONTENT PLANNER

CATEGORY:

RESOURCE LINKS:

GRAPHICS/IMAGES:

KEY POINTS:

SEO CHECKLIST:

- Primary keyword in post title
- Secondary keyword in sub-title
- Keyword in first paragraph
- Word count > 1000 words
- 1-2 Outbound Links
- Internal Link Structure
- Post URL includes keywords
- Meta description added
- Post includes images
- Post includes sub-headlines
- Social sharing enabled

NOTES:

POST PLANNER

WEEK OF: _____

TYPE: ARTICLE: ☐   TUTORIAL: ☐   REVIEW: ☐   GUEST POST: ☐

PUBLICATION DATE:

TITLE:
CATEGORY:
KEYWORDS:
NOTES:

PUBLICATION DATE:

TITLE:
CATEGORY:
KEYWORDS:
NOTES:

PUBLICATION DATE:

TITLE:
CATEGORY:
KEYWORDS:
NOTES:

POST PLANNER

WEEK OF: _____

TYPE: ARTICLE: ☐ TUTORIAL: ☐ REVIEW: ☐ GUEST POST: ☐

PUBLICATION DATE:

TITLE:

CATEGORY:

KEYWORDS:

NOTES:

LIST BUILDING PROGRESS:

 # SUBSCRIBERS: _____ **EMAILED THIS WEEK** ✉

SOCIAL MEDIA PROMO THIS WEEK:

Twitter Facebook Pinterest Instagram YouTube LinkedIn Google+

EXTERNAL LINKS:

PRODUCTS PROMOTED:

INTERNAL LINKS:

Affiliate Disclaimer Included

MARKETING PLANNER

TOP TRAFFIC CHANNELS:

MARKETING TO DO LIST:

FREE ADVERTISING IDEAS:

PAID ADVERTISING IDEAS:

MARKETING PLANNER

PROMOTIONAL STRATEGIES TO MAXIMIZE EXPOSURE

PROMOTIONAL IDEAS:

MARKETING TO DO:

SOCIAL MEDIA GROWTH TRACKER:

	BEFORE:	AFTER:
Facebook		
Instagram		
Twitter		
Pinterest		
YouTube		

OTHER:

LIST BUILDING & ENGAGEMENT:

- MAILING LIST SUBSCRIBERS:
- # OF EMAILS SENT TO SUBSCRIBERS:
- # OF NEW BLOG POSTS THIS WEEK:
- # OF COMPLETED GUEST POSTS:

NOTES:

GUEST BLOGGING

POST TITLE:

PUBLISH DATE:	CATEGORY:

MAIN TOPIC:

POST SUMMARY:

KEY POINTS:

INCLUDED LINKS:

SHARED ON:
- FACEBOOK
- INSTAGRAM
- TWITTER
- PINTEREST

TAGS & KEYWORDS:

OF COMMENTS: # OF TRACKBACKS:

NOTES:

OCTOBER

TASKS, MARKETING, ENGAGEMENT & MONETIZATION

CONTENT IDEAS

PROMOTION IDEAS

TOP PRIORITIES

MONTHLY FOCUS

MONETIZATION IDEAS

MONTHLY GOALS

MAIN OBJECTIVE:

GOAL:

ACTION STEPS:

GOAL:

ACTION STEPS:

GOAL:

ACTION STEPS:

TRAFFIC STATS:

MAILING LIST SUBSCRIBERS:

CONTENT PLANNER

POST TITLE:

PUBLICATION DATE:

TARGETED KEYWORDS:

TO DO CHECKLIST:

- Research Topic
- Pinpoint Target Audience
- Choose target keywords
- Optimize for search engines
- Link to other blog post
- Create post images
- Proofread & Edit Post
- Schedule Post Date

SOCIAL SHARING: (circle all that apply)

Facebook · Twitter · YouTube · Pinterest · LinkedIn · Instagram

TOPIC OUTLINE:

NOTES:

CONTENT PLANNER

CATEGORY:

RESOURCE LINKS:

GRAPHICS/IMAGES:

KEY POINTS:

SEO CHECKLIST:

- [ ] Primary keyword in post title
- [ ] Secondary keyword in sub-title
- [ ] Keyword in first paragraph
- [ ] Word count > 1000 words
- [ ] 1-2 Outbound Links
- [ ] Internal Link Structure
- [ ] Post URL includes keywords
- [ ] Meta description added
- [ ] Post includes images
- [ ] Post includes sub-headlines
- [ ] Social sharing enabled

NOTES:

POST PLANNER

WEEK OF: _____

TYPE: ARTICLE: _____   TUTORIAL: _____   REVIEW: _____   GUEST POST: _____

PUBLICATION DATE:

TITLE:

CATEGORY:

KEYWORDS:

NOTES:

PUBLICATION DATE:

TITLE:

CATEGORY:

KEYWORDS:

NOTES:

PUBLICATION DATE:

TITLE:

CATEGORY:

KEYWORDS:

NOTES:

POST PLANNER

WEEK OF: _____

TYPE: ARTICLE: ☐   TUTORIAL: ☐   REVIEW: ☐   GUEST POST: ☐

PUBLICATION DATE:

TITLE:

CATEGORY:

KEYWORDS:

NOTES:

LIST BUILDING PROGRESS:

 # SUBSCRIBERS: _____   **EMAILED THIS WEEK** ✉

SOCIAL MEDIA PROMO THIS WEEK:

☐ Twitter   ☐ Facebook   ☐ Pinterest   ☐ Instagram   ☐ YouTube   ☐ LinkedIn   ☐ Google+

EXTERNAL LINKS:

PRODUCTS PROMOTED:

INTERNAL LINKS:

☐ Affiliate Disclaimer Included

MARKETING PLANNER

TOP TRAFFIC CHANNELS:

MARKETING TO DO LIST:

FREE ADVERTISING IDEAS:

PAID ADVERTISING IDEAS:

MARKETING PLANNER

PROMOTIONAL STRATEGIES TO MAXIMIZE EXPOSURE

PROMOTIONAL IDEAS:

MARKETING TO DO:

SOCIAL MEDIA GROWTH TRACKER:

	BEFORE:	AFTER:
Facebook		
Instagram		
Twitter		
Pinterest		
YouTube		

OTHER:

LIST BUILDING & ENGAGEMENT:

- MAILING LIST SUBSCRIBERS:
- # OF EMAILS SENT TO SUBSCRIBERS:
- # OF NEW BLOG POSTS THIS WEEK:
- # OF COMPLETED GUEST POSTS:

NOTES:

GUEST BLOGGING

POST TITLE:

PUBLISH DATE:

CATEGORY:

MAIN TOPIC:

POST SUMMARY:

KEY POINTS:

INCLUDED LINKS:

SHARED ON:
FACEBOOK   INSTAGRAM
TWITTER   PINTEREST

TAGS & KEYWORDS:

OF COMMENTS: # OF TRACKBACKS:

NOTES:

NOVEMBER

TASKS, MARKETING, ENGAGEMENT & MONETIZATION

CONTENT IDEAS

PROMOTION IDEAS

TOP PRIORITIES

MONTHLY FOCUS

MONETIZATION IDEAS

MONTHLY GOALS

MAIN OBJECTIVE:

GOAL:

ACTION STEPS:

GOAL:

ACTION STEPS:

GOAL:

ACTION STEPS:

TRAFFIC STATS:

MAILING LIST SUBSCRIBERS:

CONTENT PLANNER

POST TITLE:

PUBLICATION DATE:

TARGETED KEYWORDS:

TO DO CHECKLIST:

- Research Topic
- Pinpoint Target Audience
- Choose target keywords
- Optimize for search engines
- Link to other blog post
- Create post images
- Proofread & Edit Post
- Schedule Post Date

SOCIAL SHARING: (circle all that apply)

Facebook Twitter YouTube Pinterest LinkedIn Instagram

TOPIC OUTLINE:

NOTES:

CONTENT PLANNER

CATEGORY:

RESOURCE LINKS:

GRAPHICS/IMAGES:

KEY POINTS:

SEO CHECKLIST:

- Primary keyword in post title
- Secondary keyword in sub-title
- Keyword in first paragraph
- Word count > 1000 words
- 1-2 Outbound Links
- Internal Link Structure
- Post URL includes keywords
- Meta description added
- Post includes images
- Post includes sub-headlines
- Social sharing enabled

NOTES:

POST PLANNER

WEEK OF: _____

TYPE: ARTICLE: ☐   TUTORIAL: ☐   REVIEW: ☐   GUEST POST: ☐

PUBLICATION DATE:

TITLE: _____

CATEGORY: _____

KEYWORDS: _____

NOTES: _____

PUBLICATION DATE:

TITLE: _____

CATEGORY: _____

KEYWORDS: _____

NOTES: _____

PUBLICATION DATE:

TITLE: _____

CATEGORY: _____

KEYWORDS: _____

NOTES: _____

POST PLANNER

WEEK OF: _____

TYPE: ARTICLE: TUTORIAL: REVIEW: GUEST POST:

PUBLICATION DATE:

TITLE:

CATEGORY:

KEYWORDS:

NOTES:

LIST BUILDING PROGRESS:

 # SUBSCRIBERS: EMAILED THIS WEEK ✉

SOCIAL MEDIA PROMO THIS WEEK:

🐦 Twitter   f Facebook   P Pinterest   📷 Instagram   ▶ YouTube   in LinkedIn   g+ Google+

EXTERNAL LINKS: **PRODUCTS PROMOTED:**

INTERNAL LINKS:

Affiliate Disclaimer Included

POST PLANNER

WEEK OF: _____

TYPE: ARTICLE: ☐ TUTORIAL: ☐ REVIEW: ☐ GUEST POST: ☐

PUBLICATION DATE:

TITLE:

CATEGORY:

KEYWORDS:

NOTES:

LIST BUILDING PROGRESS:

SUBSCRIBERS: _____   EMAILED THIS WEEK ✉

SOCIAL MEDIA PROMO THIS WEEK:

☐ Twitter ☐ Facebook ☐ Pinterest ☐ Instagram ☐ YouTube ☐ LinkedIn ☐ Google+

EXTERNAL LINKS:

PRODUCTS PROMOTED:

INTERNAL LINKS:

☐ Affiliate Disclaimer Included

MARKETING PLANNER

TOP TRAFFIC CHANNELS:

MARKETING TO DO LIST:

FREE ADVERTISING IDEAS:

PAID ADVERTISING IDEAS:

MARKETING PLANNER

PROMOTIONAL STRATEGIES TO MAXIMIZE EXPOSURE

PROMOTIONAL IDEAS:

MARKETING TO DO:

SOCIAL MEDIA GROWTH TRACKER:

	BEFORE:	AFTER:
Facebook		
Instagram		
Twitter		
Pinterest		
YouTube		

OTHER:

LIST BUILDING & ENGAGEMENT:

- MAILING LIST SUBSCRIBERS:
- # OF EMAILS SENT TO SUBSCRIBERS:
- # OF NEW BLOG POSTS THIS WEEK:
- # OF COMPLETED GUEST POSTS:

NOTES:

GUEST BLOGGING

POST TITLE:

PUBLISH DATE:

CATEGORY:

MAIN TOPIC:

POST SUMMARY:

KEY POINTS:

INCLUDED LINKS:

SHARED ON:
FACEBOOK   INSTAGRAM
TWITTER   PINTEREST

TAGS & KEYWORDS:

OF COMMENTS: # OF TRACKBACKS:

NOTES:

DECEMBER

TASKS, MARKETING, ENGAGEMENT & MONETIZATION

CONTENT IDEAS

PROMOTION IDEAS

TOP PRIORITIES

MONTHLY FOCUS

MONETIZATION IDEAS

MONTHLY GOALS

MAIN OBJECTIVE:

GOAL:

ACTION STEPS:

GOAL:

ACTION STEPS:

GOAL:

ACTION STEPS:

TRAFFIC STATS:

MAILING LIST SUBSCRIBERS:

CONTENT PLANNER

POST TITLE:

PUBLICATION DATE:

TARGETED KEYWORDS:

TO DO CHECKLIST:

- Research Topic
- Pinpoint Target Audience
- Choose target keywords
- Optimize for search engines
- Link to other blog post
- Create post images
- Proofread & Edit Post
- Schedule Post Date

SOCIAL SHARING: (circle all that apply)

Facebook · Twitter · YouTube · Pinterest · LinkedIn · Instagram

TOPIC OUTLINE:

NOTES:

CONTENT PLANNER

CATEGORY:

RESOURCE LINKS:

GRAPHICS/IMAGES:

KEY POINTS:

SEO CHECKLIST:

- Primary keyword in post title
- Secondary keyword in sub-title
- Keyword in first paragraph
- Word count > 1000 words
- 1-2 Outbound Links
- Internal Link Structure
- Post URL includes keywords
- Meta description added
- Post includes images
- Post includes sub-headlines
- Social sharing enabled

NOTES:

POST PLANNER

WEEK OF: _____

TYPE: ARTICLE: ☐   TUTORIAL: ☐   REVIEW: ☐   GUEST POST: ☐

PUBLICATION DATE:

TITLE:

CATEGORY:

KEYWORDS:

NOTES:

PUBLICATION DATE:

TITLE:

CATEGORY:

KEYWORDS:

NOTES:

PUBLICATION DATE:

TITLE:

CATEGORY:

KEYWORDS:

NOTES:

POST PLANNER

WEEK OF: _____

TYPE: ARTICLE: ☐ TUTORIAL: ☐ REVIEW: ☐ GUEST POST: ☐

PUBLICATION DATE:

TITLE:

CATEGORY:

KEYWORDS:

NOTES:

LIST BUILDING PROGRESS:

 # SUBSCRIBERS: _____ **EMAILED THIS WEEK** ✉

SOCIAL MEDIA PROMO THIS WEEK:

☐ Twitter ☐ Facebook ☐ Pinterest ☐ Instagram ☐ YouTube ☐ LinkedIn ☐ Google+

EXTERNAL LINKS:

PRODUCTS PROMOTED:

INTERNAL LINKS:

Affiliate Disclaimer Included

MARKETING PLANNER

TOP TRAFFIC CHANNELS:

MARKETING TO DO LIST:

FREE ADVERTISING IDEAS:

PAID ADVERTISING IDEAS:

MARKETING PLANNER

PROMOTIONAL STRATEGIES TO MAXIMIZE EXPOSURE

PROMOTIONAL IDEAS:

MARKETING TO DO:

SOCIAL MEDIA GROWTH TRACKER:

	BEFORE:	AFTER:
Facebook		
Instagram		
Twitter		
Pinterest		
YouTube		

OTHER:

LIST BUILDING & ENGAGEMENT:

- MAILING LIST SUBSCRIBERS:
- # OF EMAILS SENT TO SUBSCRIBERS:
- # OF NEW BLOG POSTS THIS WEEK:
- # OF COMPLETED GUEST POSTS:

NOTES:

GUEST BLOGGING

POST TITLE:

PUBLISH DATE:

CATEGORY:

MAIN TOPIC:

POST SUMMARY:

KEY POINTS:

INCLUDED LINKS:

SHARED ON:

FACEBOOK

INSTAGRAM

TWITTER

PINTEREST

TAGS & KEYWORDS:

OF COMMENTS:

OF TRACKBACKS:

NOTES:

CPSIA information can be obtained
at www.ICGtesting.com
Printed in the USA
LVHW061252260819
628843LV00018B/122/P